Orca
Origins

Monique Polak

PASSOVER

Festival of Freedom

ORCA BOOK PUBLISHERS

Library and Archives Canada Cataloguing in Publication

Polak, Monique, author
Passover: festival of freedom / Monique Polak.
(Orca origins)

Includes index.

Issued in print and electronic formats.
ISBN 978-1-4598-0990-1 (bound).—ISBN 978-1-4598-0991-8 (pdf).—
ISBN 978-1-4598-0992-5 (epub)

1. Passover—Juvenile literature. I. Title.
BM695.P3P64 2016   j296.4'37   C2015-904482-0
                         C2015-904483-9

First published in the United States, 2016
Library of Congress Control Number: 2015944491

Summary: Enlivened by personal stories, *Passover* illuminates and celebrates how ancient Jewish traditions are kept alive in the modern world in this work of nonfiction for middle readers.

Orca Book Publishers is dedicated to preserving the environment and has printed this book on Forest Stewardship Council® certified paper.

Orca Book Publishers gratefully acknowledges the support for its publishing programs provided by the following agencies: the Government of Canada through the Canada Book Fund and the Canada Council for the Arts, and the Province of British Columbia through the BC Arts Council and the Book Publishing Tax Credit.

Design by Rachel Page
Front cover photos by PhotoStock-Israel.com, Dreamstime.com, Shari Nakagawa, Shutterstock.com, iStock.com
Back cover photo by iStock.com

ORCA BOOK PUBLISHERS
www.orcabook.com

Printed and bound in Canada.

19 18 17 16 • 4 3 2 1

To Carolyn, sister and friend

CONTENTS

7 Introduction

Chapter One:
What's Passover All About?

10 The Passover Story
13 Celebrating Passover
15 The Seder Meal
17 The Ten Plagues
22 Ben's Story (Part One)

Chapter Two:
Passover Before and After the Holocaust

24 Ben's Story (Part Two)
29 Liselotte's Story
36 Passover 1943: The Warsaw Ghetto Uprising

Chapter Three:
Passover in Action

38 Kids and Passover
39 Passover and the Obligation to Do Good
40 Montreal Food Baskets
45 Passover Food Drive
46 Kehila Jewish Community Day School
47 The Friendship Circle
48 King David High School

Chapter Four:
Passover Around the World

50 Every Seder Has Its Own Flavor

51 Israel

53 The Netherlands

54 China

54 Nepal

55 Italy

57 Ukraine

58 Ethiopia

59 Iraq

60 Morocco

64 A Final Word from the Author

65 *Glossary*

67 *References and Resources*

69 *Index*

72 *Acknowledgments*

Praying at the Western Wall in Israel.
flik47/iStock.com

Passover table.
PhotoStock-Israel.com

Introduction

When I was growing up, I often attended the **Passover seder** at my friend Debbi's house. Debbi lived around the corner from us in Côte Saint-Luc, a Montreal suburb that was, in the 1960s and '70s, predominantly Jewish.

I was mostly interested in the food—the cracker-y **matzo**, the chicken soup with matzo balls, the brisket and the roast chicken. Because I don't speak **Hebrew**, there were many parts of the Passover story I did not understand. And to be honest, I didn't pay much attention to the parts of the story that Debbi's father told us in English.

Though my own family is Jewish, we are not observant. Growing up, we hardly ever went to **synagogue** (a Jewish house of worship), nor did we observe the holidays or keep a **kosher** home, meaning we did not follow

Matzo ball soup is a staple at the seder meal.
Patrick Heagney/iStock.com

> Like Christianity and Islam, Judaism is monotheistic, which means that Jews believe in one god.

Jewish dietary laws. In part, that could be because during the **Holocaust**, my mother, Celien, who comes from the Netherlands, spent nearly three years in a Nazi **concentration camp**. She was not an observant Jew before the Holocaust, but she was even less interested in religion afterward. "If there is a God," she once said to me, "how could He have let the Holocaust happen?"

So, until now, my own connection to Judaism has focused mostly on the Holocaust. At Marianopolis College, where I teach in Montreal, I have taught courses on Holocaust literature. In 2008, I wrote a novel for young adults based on my mother's wartime experiences— stories she kept secret for more than sixty years.

But when I was asked to write this book about Passover, I agreed immediately. That's because I knew it was time to broaden my own understanding of Jewish history and religion.

Ultra-Orthodox Jews preparing for Passover.
kobbydagan/iStock.com

I live in Montreal, a city where many Holocaust survivors settled. Like my mother, who is now 86, these Holocaust survivors are reaching the end of their lives. As part of my research for this book, I spoke with dozens of people about what Passover means to them. Two of the people I interviewed are also Holocaust survivors—Ben Younger and Liselotte Ivry.

Learning about Passover and hearing so many stories about this holiday has deepened my connection to my religion and to the Jewish people who came before me. That is why in 2015, for the first time, I hosted the Passover seder at my house.

When I was growing up, my family and I did not celebrate Passover. This family picture was taken in 2015. I'm in the beige sweater, wearing glasses, and I'm with my parents, Celien and Maximilien Polak; my brother Michael (blue shirt); my sister Carolyn (at the right); and some of my nephews and nieces—Jennifer and Jason Beveridge (at the back); Lauren Abrams (in pink and yellow); Erica Lighter (also in beige) and Claudia Lighter (at the front).
Courtesy Monique Polak

ONE

WHAT'S PASSOVER ALL ABOUT?

This matzo is made by hand. Today, square matzo is more common.

ChameleonsEye/Shutterstock.com

The Passover Story

Every spring, Jewish families around the world gather to celebrate Passover. At special holiday meals called seders, Jewish families say prayers, drink wine (grape juice for the kids), and eat foods such as matzo. But most importantly, Jews retell the remarkable story of Passover.

Matzo—a bread made without yeast—is not the only special food eaten at Passover. In fact, of all the holidays on the Jewish calendar, Passover has the greatest number of symbolic foods and rituals.

By retelling the Passover story year after year, Jews are reminded how, more than 3,000 years ago, their ancestors emerged from slavery to become free men and women.

The Passover story reminds us that the freedom to be who we are and to practice our religion, whatever that may be, is a great gift. It also teaches us that if we summon our courage and look out for each other, we can endure and overcome the most challenging circumstances.

According to biblical scholars, the story of Passover began sometime between 1300 and 1200 BCE (Before the Common Era). During this period, the Jews, who were known then as Israelites, lived in Egypt. The ruler of ancient Egypt was called the pharaoh. There were pharaohs who treated the Israelites kindly, but at the time the Passover story began, the pharaoh who ruled over Egypt was a cruel man who mistreated the Israelites. There is some disagreement about the name of this cruel pharaoh, but biblical commentary suggests he was Merneptah, son of Ramesses II. Merneptah forced the Jews into slavery, making them do hard labor from early morning until late at night. Imagine grueling workdays spent in the hot sun, hauling the giant stones needed to build the great pyramids. If the Israelites did not work hard enough, they were beaten.

The Israelites could not continue living under these conditions. More than anything else, they longed for freedom. So Moses, their leader, went to the pharaoh to ask permission for the Israelites to leave Egypt so they could make their way to the **promised land**, now called Israel.

The pharaoh refused.

Because God was angry with the pharaoh for not setting the Israelites free, he punished the pharaoh by sending a series of plagues, or calamities, upon Egypt.

Still the pharaoh did not relent. He refused to grant the Israelites their freedom.

"Passover affirms the great truth that liberty is the inalienable right of every human being."

—*Rabbi Morris Joseph, 1848–1930, author of Judaism as Creed and Life*

In Toronto, siblings Emmanuella and Sam Gladman dress up as Egyptians and re-enact the Passover story.
Courtesy Jessica Naves Gladman

Passover Facts

Who Was Moses?

Before Moses's birth, the pharaoh decreed that every Israelite baby boy be killed. So Moses's mother put him in a basket and sent the basket floating down the Nile River.

The pharaoh's daughter found Moses and raised him in the pharaoh's court. When Moses was much older, he killed a guard for beating an Israelite. The pharaoh wanted Moses killed, but Moses fled to the desert.

Forty years later, Moses was in the desert when he saw a burning bush and heard God's voice. God told Moses: "Deliver my people from Egypt to the promised land."

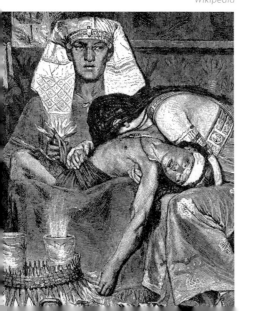

Death of the Pharaoh's Firstborn, by Dutch-born painter Sir Lawrence Alma-Tadema.
Wikipedia

Until God sent his tenth plague.

For his tenth plague, God sent his Angel of Death to kill the firstborn son of every Egyptian family. Even the pharaoh's.

But God spared the Israelites, warning them to mark their doorposts with the blood of a lamb so that the Angel of Death would know to *pass over* their homes. This explains the origin of the word *Passover*.

Only when the Angel of Death killed the pharaoh's first-born son did the pharaoh finally relent and agree to give the Israelites their freedom and allow them to leave Egypt. But after all that had happened, the pharaoh was furious. He told the Israelites, "You must leave immediately!"

The Israelites did not even have time to wait for their bread dough to rise. So they packed the dough in their sacks and it baked in the hot sun, becoming matzo. This explains why, during Passover, Jews eat matzo instead of bread.

Though the Israelites were now free to leave Egypt, their struggles were not over. Soon after the Israelites left Egypt, the pharaoh had a change of heart. He sent his soldiers after the Israelites, to bring them back and return them to slavery. The pharaoh's soldiers arrived just as the Israelites reached the Red Sea. They were sure they were trapped. But then a miracle happened—the waters parted, allowing the Israelites to cross the sea on foot, without even getting a little bit wet. And when the pharaoh's soldiers tried to follow, the waters came crashing over them and they drowned.

But still the Israelites struggled, wandering in the wilderness for forty years. It is believed they wandered so long because they still had a slave mentality and their faith in God was not strong enough. Even so, during their many years of wandering, God looked after the Israelites. When they ran out of food, God poured down bread, or **manna**, from the heavens.

Perhaps the length of their journey shows us that the transformation from being a slave to a free man or woman does not happen in a flash. Genuine change, especially the kind that involves a change in how we see ourselves, cannot be rushed.

Celebrating Passover

The Passover holiday lasts eight days (seven days in Israel), but preparations begin well in advance.

First, the house is cleaned and every trace of bread or flour is removed. In the olden days, the bread was burned.

Crossing of the Red Sea, by French painter Nicolas Poussin.
Wikipedia

Today, some ultra-Orthodox Jews still burn their bread in preparation for Passover.
alexkuehni/iStock.com

Israeli kindergarten children preparing matzo.
Wikipedia

Some ultra-Orthodox Jews still burn their bread before Passover. But today, most Jews try to use up all the bread before Passover so nothing is wasted.

A special meal called the seder marks the beginning of Passover. In fact, in most parts of the world, there are two seders—on the first and second nights of Passover. In Hebrew, the word *seder* means "order." Order is an important part of the Passover seder. There is a certain order of events that is always followed.

This order of events is set out in a Jewish book called the **Haggadah**. Copies of the Haggadah are passed around the dinner table so that everyone can take part in the service and in retelling the Passover story. *Haggadah* is Hebrew for "to tell," reminding Jews of their obligation to tell the Passover story to their children.

The seder plate is another important part of the Passover meal. On the plate are six foods that serve as symbols to help us tell the Passover story. A roasted shank bone reminds us of the *Paschal* (or Passover) lamb sacrificed by our ancestors and offered on the altar of the great Temple in Jerusalem at Passover. A hard-boiled egg, like the Paschal lamb, was also offered in the great Temple at Passover. **Maror** comes from the Hebrew word *mar*, meaning "bitter," to remind us of the bitterness of slavery. The two bitter herbs on the seder plate are usually horseradish (**hazeret** in Hebrew), and romaine lettuce. **Charoset**, a sweet-tasting paste made from fruit and nuts, symbolizes the mortar our ancestors used to make bricks when they were slaves in Egypt. Finally, there is **karpas**, a green vegetable—usually parsley or celery that has been dipped in salt water. This vegetable symbolizes the arrival of spring and reminds us to give thanks for the gifts we receive from the earth. When we shake the salt water from the parsley or celery, the droplets recall the tears our ancestors shed when they were slaves.

And of course, there is the matzo. Three matzos, placed in the folds of a large napkin or matzo cover, remind us of our ancestors' hasty departure from Egypt.

The Seder Meal

The seder begins with a blessing or prayer called the **Kiddush**, usually recited by the head of the family. In the Kiddush, Passover is referred to as the "Feast of Unleavened Bread," and we bless God and thank him for giving us holidays like Passover. This is also the time to drink from the first glass of wine (or grape juice).

Next comes a part of the ceremony known as **Urchatz**, which means "washing of the hands." Two guests,

Four friends read from the Haggadah at a Seder in Delft, the Netherlands. From left to right: Daniel Lev, Jeremy Even, Alon Topper and Judith Lev.
Courtesy of Bianca Even-Roberti

A traditional seder plate containing all six symbolic foods.
iStock.com

The seder begins with a blessing or prayer called the Kiddush.
tovfla/iStock.com

For most kids, the search for the afikoman is the highlight of the seder.
PhotoStock-Israel.com

often children, bring a pitcher of water, a bowl and a towel. The guests pour some water over their hands into the bowl. Urchatz is a symbolic act of purification.

Now it is time for karpas. The head of the family gives each guest a piece of green vegetable, which the guests dip into salt water. Together, the guests recite a prayer in which they express their gratitude to God for having created the "fruit of the earth." This prayer also remembers the ancient Israelites who were enslaved in Egypt.

The next part of the ceremony is called **Yachatz**. The head of the family takes the three matzos from the seder plate and breaks the middle matzo in two. When the children are not looking, he hides one half of that matzo (called the **afikoman**). Popular hiding spots are under a pillow or blanket. The children will hunt for the afikoman when it is time for dessert. Once the afikoman is hidden, there is a prayer over the matzos. This prayer invites those who are hungry to share the seder meal. Now it is time to refill the wine cups.

Now come the four questions, or **Mah Nishtanah**, a part of the seder meal that kids like a lot. That is because it is customary for the youngest child at the table to ask the four questions (see the sidebar to learn more about the four questions)—as long as he or she is old enough to speak. Sometimes the child has memorized the questions, and sometimes he or she reads them. Other times an older child may need to help a younger one read. The four questions allow children to participate in the seder but, of course, the questions—and their answers—provide a kind of mini-lesson about the history of Passover.

There are still more stories to tell at the seder. These include the stories of the Four Sons: one who was wise, one who was wicked, one who was simple and one who was too young to come up with questions. There is also the story of how the Israelites came to Egypt, how they were enslaved and how Moses led them to freedom.

It's time now for the story of the ten plagues.

The Ten Plagues

1. First, God turned the waters of Egypt to blood, making all the fish die and the water undrinkable. Only the Israelites had fish to eat and clear water to drink.
2. Hordes of frogs swarmed over every inch of Egypt. Only the Israelites were not bothered by the frogs.
3. Lice invaded all the homes in Egypt—except for the homes of the Israelites.
4. Wild animals caused great havoc and destruction, and only the Israelites were spared.

Passover Facts

The Four Questions— and Their Answers

1. **Why is it on this night we eat matzo?**

   We eat matzo to remind us that our ancestors did not have time to bake bread as they hurried out of Egypt.

2. **Why is it on this night we eat bitter herbs?**

   We eat bitter herbs to remind us of the bitterness of slavery.

3. **Why is it on this night we dip (wash our hands) twice?**

   We dip twice to replace our tears with gratitude and to sweeten bitterness and suffering.

4. **Why is it on this night we eat reclining?**

   We eat reclining to demonstrate that we are free men, women and children.

The Plague of Frogs. Colored etching in the Wellcome Collection, London, England.
Wikipedia

My nieces, Lauren (left) and Claudia (right), show off their seder plate.
Courtesy Monique Polak

5. God sent a pestilence. All of the livestock—the horses, the cows, the sheep and the goats— suddenly grew ill, but not the livestock that belonged to the Israelites.

6. Painful red sores called boils covered the bodies of every Egyptian, but not the bodies of the Israelites.

7. And then there was hail that fell from the sky and destroyed all of the crops in Egypt, except for the crops that belonged to the Israelites.

8. Then came locusts that devoured whatever food was still left after the hailstorms.

9. After the locusts there was a terrible, unrelenting darkness. For three days straight, all of Egypt remained dark as night.

10. The tenth and final plague was the worst: God killed the firstborn son of every Egyptian family.

As each plague is named, the guests dip a finger into their glass of wine and let a droplet fall onto a saucer. These droplets are a way to remember the effect of the plagues on the Egyptians. Though the Israelites regained their freedom, they acknowledged that their enemies had suffered too. According to the Haggadah, a full cup of wine symbolizes complete happiness. So the droplets on our saucers reveal that our happiness is incomplete when there are others who suffered in order for us to achieve happiness.

Now guests join together to sing "**Dayenu**" (Hebrew for "we are grateful"). In the song, Jews thank God for his loving kindness and for performing such miracles as dividing the Red Sea and sending manna from heaven when our ancestors journeyed through the wilderness.

When the song is over, it is time to talk about the significance of the shank bone, the matzo and the bitter herbs.

The Plague of Hail and Thunder. Colored etching in the Wellcome Collection, London, England.
Wikipedia

At the seder, the second washing of hands is accompanied by a blessing.

Philip Folsom

Then we raise our wine cups again and remember that the struggle for freedom is never really over. As the Haggadah tells us, "The struggle for freedom is a continuous struggle. For never does man reach total liberty and opportunity."

It is almost time to eat. First we must wash our hands a second time as we say another blessing—this time in silence. The head of the family takes the upper matzo, and the remainder of the middle matzo, and breaks them into pieces so everyone can have a piece. By now, everyone is pretty hungry, so that piece of matzo tastes extra-delicious.

The head of the family explains the meaning of the last two items on the seder plate—the maror and the charoset. Then dinner is served!

As you can imagine, with so many rituals, the Passover seder can last several hours. That may be why the search

When they pray, Jewish men (and many women) wear a head covering (in Hebrew, the kippah; in Yiddish, the yarmulke) as a sign of respect for God.

for the afikoman happens only at dessert—because it is the perfect way to keep children awake. The children hunt all over the house for the afikoman. Whoever finds it gets a reward—usually money or candy. Sometimes both!

After the meal, there is another prayer, and the wine glasses are refilled and we drink again. We bless God's name and ask for his protection.

But the seder is not quite over. We must still honor the prophet Elijah. According to ancient Jewish legends, Elijah is supposed to lift our spirits and give us hope when we feel down. The guests stand up and one person opens the front door of the house. The door is left ajar so Elijah's spirit may enter, and we say another prayer. The door is closed, the guests take their seats and the cups are refilled again. There is a cup for Elijah too.

Following this order of events unites us with our ancestors—who celebrated in much the same way—as well as with future generations who will continue the Passover rituals.

> "All of us human beings want freedom and the right to determine our own destiny as individuals and as peoples. That is human nature."
>
> —*The Dalai Lama, from his Nobel Prize acceptance speech, 1989*

Recipe for Charoset

You Will Need:

3 tart apples, such as Granny Smiths, peeled and cut into tiny pieces

1 cup walnuts, toasted and chopped

3 tablespoons golden raisins

1 teaspoon brown sugar

1 teaspoon cinnamon

1 tablespoon honey

1 tablespoon kosher Passover red wine

Instructions:

Toss all of the ingredients together. Spread on a piece of matzo.

Charoset ingredients (clockwise from upper left): kosher wine, pears, apple, cinnamon, honey, and chopped walnuts
Wikipedia

> When making this recipe as well as the other recipes in this book, be sure an adult is around to supervise.

Door left ajar so Elijah's spirit may enter,
in Neve Tzedek, Tel Aviv.
Yoav Sinai/Dreamstime.com

Ben's Story (part one)

Ben Younger in his apartment in Dollard-des-Ormeaux.
Courtesy Monique Polak

Some foods prepared for a Passover seder: (clockwise from top) matzo, parsley, horseradish, charoset.
Wikipedia

Benzion Younger is nearly 90, but when he remembers celebrating Passover as a child in Romania, his brown eyes shine like a boy's. Somehow, when I listen to his story, I see past Benzion's lined face and the bald patches on his scalp. The more he tells, the easier it is to imagine Benzion, who has used the name Ben since he immigrated to Canada in 1948, as a mischievous boy growing up in a loving, tight-knit family.

"Passover was the nicest holiday for me. Because of the food. It was the best food ever," Ben says.

Because Ben's father raised geese in the small town of Sapinta, the family often ate goose at Passover. And of course, there was always matzo, the unleavened bread eaten by Jews around the world during the Passover festival.

In Sapinta, where Ben lived until he was 17, there was a special bakery that opened only for Passover. Local Jewish families placed their orders for matzo well in advance of the holiday. Ben's mother, Ruchel, always ordered twenty kilograms (44 pounds) of matzo—enough for herself and her husband, Gitman; their three children (Ben had two younger sisters, Perl and Raizele); and her mother, Ben's grandmother, Esther Ita, who lived with the family.

Ben remembers accompanying his mother to the bakery. "My mother brought a white bed sheet to collect the matzo. When we got home, she tied the four corners of the sheet together and hung it from the ceiling so the matzo wouldn't break. We stood on a chair to reach the matzo," he said.

It is not only Ben's memories of matzo that make his eyes shine. The same thing happens when Ben recalls sitting at the seder table and listening to his father

recount the biblical story behind Passover. "My father would explain how Moses led the Jewish people out of Egypt and freed us. My favorite part was when the sea parted so the Jewish people could cross," he said. "I really believed that was true."

Ben and his family reclined on pillows at the seder table. "Big pillows," he recalled. This custom is also part of the Passover tradition. Sitting, relaxed, on pillows is a sign of freedom.

A Jewish family's last Passover before World War II. In Vilnius, Lithuania.
United States Holocaust Memorial Museum courtesy of Theodore Fremont

"Passover marks the birth of a nation. Out of a mass of slaves, Moses fashioned a nation and gave them a faith."
—*Rabbi Philip S. Bernstein, 1901–1985, who helped in the resettlement of displaced European Jews after World War II*

TWO

PASSOVER BEFORE AND AFTER THE HOLOCAUST

Ben's Story (part two)

In chapter one, you met my friend Ben Younger. He is a Holocaust survivor—the only one in his immediate family. His parents, two sisters and grandmother perished.

The Holocaust shook Ben's faith in God. Though he still attends synagogue in Dollard-des-Ormeaux, the Montreal suburb where he and his wife, Doris, live, on the High Holy Days, and on Saturdays to mark the Sabbath, Ben is far less religious than he was as a boy growing up in Sapinta, Romania. "I'm not religious anymore. The Holocaust killed a lot of beliefs I had," he says.

Food plays an important role in Ben's memories of his family's Passover seders in Sapinta. Ben's favorite dish was a simple one: matzo with milk. He remembers crumbling matzo into milk, then putting the mixture on the stove

Ben Younger looking up at the only photograph he has of his father—the man wearing the fedora hat.
Courtesy Monique Polak

until it turned mushy. "It was like a cereal. I still make it sometimes, especially at Passover," he says.

When Ben was 17, he and his family were rounded up by the Nazis and deported to Auschwitz concentration camp by cattle car—a train car designed for transporting livestock, not people. This was in 1944, but even after all these years, Ben's memories of the three-day journey remain sharp. "It was a nightmare," he says. He and his fellow passengers had no food, no water, no bathroom—and no idea where they were headed.

Almost as soon as he arrived in Auschwitz, Ben was separated from his parents. Then he was sent to a shed and ordered to undress. After that, Ben's head was shaved by another Jewish prisoner. "Not only my head. They shaved everywhere else where we grew hair," Ben says.

Ben believed both his sisters had been sent to the gas chambers with his parents, but two days later, a girl he did not recognize called to him from over a fence separating

The arrival process of Hungarian Jews from the Tet Ghetto in Auschwitz-Birkenau extermination camp in 1944.
Wikipedia

In the spring of 1944, railway tracks were laid right into Auschwitz-Birkenau to prepare for the arrival of Hungarian Jews.
Wikipedia

Passover Facts

Passover in the Camps

It was almost impossible for Jewish prisoners to celebrate Passover in the concentration camps.

But not completely impossible.

In 1945—not long before the end of World War II—at a German concentration camp called Vaihingen, a Jewish prisoner named Moshe Perl managed to talk an SS guard into giving him a five-kilogram (eleven-pound) bag of flour. Moshe told the guard the flour was for making targets for target practice.

But instead, Moshe and his friends made matzo, which they hid under the shingles of the roof of their workshop.

Twenty Jewish prisoners took part in a secret seder at Vaihingen. They shared matzo and potatoes, and drank wine made from sugar and water. They even read from the Haggadah.

This simple seder is another example of resistance during the Holocaust. Those who participated knew that if they were caught, they would almost certainly be killed.

the men's and women's barracks. It was his sister Perl, though Ben did not recognize her because her head was shaved. "'Benzion,' she told me, 'take good care of yourself. Mom and Dad are no more.' Then a soldier at a watch tower yelled, 'Get away from the fence or I'll shoot!'" Ben says. That was the last time Ben saw Perl. After the war, Ben learned that Perl died in Bergen-Belsen concentration camp and was buried there in a mass grave.

After three days in Auschwitz, Ben was shipped to Warsaw, Poland, to work on a cleanup crew in what was left of the Warsaw Ghetto, a walled-in residential area where the Nazis confined hundreds of thousands of Jews during the Holocaust. There, he scrubbed bricks and chipped away at mortar.

In the summer of 1944, Ben and his uncle David were among 4,200 prisoners forced by the Nazis to march from Warsaw to Dachau concentration camp. More than half of the prisoners died on that march.

Ben spent eight days in Dachau, before being shipped to the town of Kaufering, to build a work camp. When the work was complete, Ben and his uncle were separated. They met again when Ben was transferred to another work camp. Ben remembers what bad shape his uncle was in: "'Benzion,' he told me, 'I'm dying I'm so hungry.' I broke into the kitchen and stole some raw potatoes. When I brought them to him, he opened his mouth and closed it, and he died."

Ben was liberated on April 30, 1945. He celebrated his first Passover after the war at the Bergen-Belsen displaced persons (DP) camp, located about a kilometer (less than a mile) from the concentration camp of the same name.

Ben remembers that a rabbi conducted the seder, that there were long tables loaded with food and that most of the others who attended the seder were teenagers like himself. Ben says he felt happy and sad at the same time. "That seder was extremely emotional. Everyone was singing and crying. I know I was depressed. But at the same time, I felt, 'I'm in a family...I'm back to the religious family I grew up with.'"

Ben's Holocaust experience altered his relationship with God. "Before, I always thought we Jews were special to God," he says. But even with his doubts, Ben refuses to give up his belief in God altogether. "I can't say there is no God," he tells me.

At the DP camp, Ben learned from a friend that two girls from Sapinta had also survived. The girls turned out to be Ben's cousins. They gave Ben the only photograph he has of family in Sapinta. It is a photo of Ben's father,

"I can feel the suffering of millions—and yet, if I look into the heavens, I think it will come out all right, that this cruelty too will end."

—Anne Frank, from
The Diary of Anne Frank, 1944

The Haggadah.
k45025/iStock.com

Israeli children reading the Haggadah.
Chen Leopold/PhotoStock-Israel.com

looking confident and dapper. The photo has a place of honor on the wall unit in Ben and Doris's living room.

Ben and Doris have three children and five grandchildren. "They are my everything," Ben says. "This is the greatest thing in my life."

At Passover, Ben's youngest daughter, Judy, hosts the seder at her home in Côte Saint-Luc, in Montreal's west end. "We all sing and take turns reading the Haggadah. Our youngest grandchild, Michelle, asks the four questions," Ben says.

Ben admits that hearing the Passover story sometimes leaves him feeling troubled. "The story of Passover—it hits me. I think, 'God, if you could do this to our people...how could you have allowed the Holocaust to happen?'"

Liselotte's Story

Liselotte Ivry standing in her kitchen in Montreal.
Courtesy Monique Polak

For my friend and fellow Montrealer, Liselotte Ivry, Passover is a time to celebrate the survival of the Jewish people—as well as her own survival. During the Holocaust, Liselotte was imprisoned for nearly three years in Nazi concentration camps.

Today, at the age of 90, Liselotte is fiercely independent. Widowed since 1996, she still lives in the Côte Saint-Luc split-level house where she and her husband raised their two children. She refuses my offer to take her shopping or to bring her a home-cooked meal. "I do my own cooking," she insists. "Besides, I eat kosher." Liselotte is not the sort of person who cares whether people like her. What seems to matter most to her is speaking up—and telling her story.

Liselotte was born in 1925 in what was then called Czechoslovakia (now known as the Czech Republic). As a child, Liselotte was called Lisl. She grew up in Listany, a village with a population of about 300. Because there were only four Jewish families, Listany had no synagogue. "On Jewish Holy Days, my family and I walked through meadows, woods and fields to go to synagogue in another village," Liselotte recalls. Jews and non-Jews in Listany got along well. Liselotte's parents owned a general store, which her mother continued to operate after Liselotte's father died in 1929. The store sold everything from buttons and fabric to sugar and pickled herring.

The village of Listany, where Liselotte grew up.
Wikipedia

The family home was in the same building as the store. When Liselotte was about six, she was left in charge of the store when her mother went to the city of Pilsen, some eighteen kilometers (eleven miles) away, to buy merchandise. "If someone wanted something and we did not have it, I wrote down what it was so my mother could order it," says Liselotte. "I felt very important." Liselotte used to enjoy dipping into the store's chocolate supply. "We had a chocolate layered with fruits and figs. My mother didn't sell an ounce—because I ate it all," Liselotte says, chuckling at the memory.

Every year, Liselotte looked forward to Passover. She remembers that her mother ordered matzo from a factory in Pardubice. "It was the only place in Bohemia that made matzo," Liselotte says. The matzo was round and came in five-kilogram (eleven-pound) packages, wrapped in white paper. Liselotte's mother would leave one package on the counter in the store. "Every customer got a free matzo," Liselotte recalls.

At Passover, Liselotte's mother made a special delicacy called **matzo loksh**—a noodle pudding made from matzo, eggs and goose fat. She served the matzo loksh with a sauce made with wine, egg yolks and sugar. Liselotte delivered bowls of matzo loksh to her non-Jewish neighbors. "It was our custom every year to bring them this dish. They would be waiting for it when I arrived," Liselotte recalls.

Back then, it was customary for a man to conduct the seder, so after Liselotte's father's death, Liselotte, her mother and her little brother, Hanus, attended the seder at the home of a neighbor. When the neighbor died, the family shared the seder meal with friends in Pilsen. They traveled there by horse and buggy. "We were excited to be going to the seder," says Liselotte.

Liselotte's life was turned upside down when, in 1938, the Nazis invaded the region known then as the Sudetenland, the Czech borderland where Listany was located. "In the middle of the night, there was a knock on our door. It was a Czech officer who wanted to buy gasoline. He told us they were leaving because the Germans

"I don't call myself a survivor. I call myself a witness to history."
—Liselotte Ivry,
Holocaust survivor

Liselotte, with her mother and little brother, Hanus.
Courtesy Liselotte Ivry

After the Holocaust, girls eating matzo during Passover at the Rothschild Centre in Vienna, Austria.

Yad Vashem

were coming to take over," Liselotte recalls. Liselotte's mother asked the officer whether she and the children could come along—and he agreed. There was only time to pack a few things.

First, the family spent a few days with relatives in Tremosna, a village near Pilsen that had not been occupied by the Germans. Afterward, they went to Prague, the Czech capital, where Liselotte's aunts and uncles lived. "It was turmoil. I remember our relatives meeting us at the train station," says Liselotte.

Liselotte, her mother and Hanus were separated. Hanus lived with cousins, Liselotte's mother with her sister and brother, and Liselotte with another aunt and uncle. Liselotte had grown up speaking German. Now she had to learn Czech in a hurry so that she could attend the local high school.

On March 15, 1939, Liselotte was going home from school for lunch when the German tanks rolled into Prague. "On that day, my life changed forever. Though I

In 1941, Jewish prisoners at Gurs, a French detention camp, produced their own handwritten Haggadah so they could celebrate Passover. That Haggadah is now housed in the archives at Yad Vashem, Israel's official memorial to victims of the Holocaust.

was allowed to finish the school year, I wasn't allowed in a park—or on a sidewalk," she says.

In 1942, Liselotte, her mother and Hanus were deported to a concentration camp called Theresienstadt. Liselotte spent fifteen months there. "Somehow, we kept track, so we always knew when there were Jewish holidays," she says.

In 1943, Liselotte, her mother and Hanus were sent to Auschwitz. Liselotte remembers that the Nazis were especially cruel around the Jewish holidays. "The Nazis always picked the holidays for destruction," she says. Hanus was one of 4,000 Czech Jews murdered in 1944 on **Erev Purim**. Generally considered the most joyful holiday on the Jewish calendar, Purim always brings back painful memories for Liselotte. Hanus was 16 when he was sent to the gas chambers in Auschwitz.

Liselotte's mother also perished in Auschwitz. Somehow—Liselotte is not sure how—she managed to survive. "When you are a young girl, you try to work. You have to be able to live, to make it," she says.

Not long after Hanus's death, Liselotte remembers having to march by the notorious Nazi doctor Josef Mengele, who selected which prisoners were strong enough to work and which prisoners would be gassed. Prisoners who looked weak or showed signs of illness were sent to the gas chambers. "We had to file past Mengele naked, with our clothes held over our right arms. That was because they had to see the numbers tattooed on our left arms. I suffer from psoriasis (a chronic skin condition), but that day, I didn't have a pimple. God was with me," Liselotte says. Had Liselotte's psoriasis been visible, it is likely that Mengele would have sent her to her death.

After seven months in Auschwitz, Liselotte was sent to Tiefstack concentration camp in Hamburg, to build bombs. From Tiefstack, Liselotte was sent to Bergen-Belsen, the concentration camp from which she was liberated in April 1945.

Liselotte cherishes her memories of the Passovers she celebrated after liberation: "We lost so much. But by celebrating holidays like Passover, we remind ourselves of what it means to be Jews. If we give up our customs, then nothing was worth surviving for."

Liselotte's uncle Gustav Sicher, a rabbi and professor of philosophy, and his wife, Elsa, who had lived in Prague, managed to escape the Holocaust by moving to Palestine. But the couple returned to Prague after the war when Gustav was offered a position as the city's chief rabbi. "They made a fantastic seder. People came from all over," Liselotte says.

Liselotte remembers how Uncle Gustav sat at the head of the table wearing a white garment called a **kitl** and a high kippah, or skullcap. "The seder lasted until three in

Liselotte's uncle Gustav Sicher returned from Palestine after World War II to become chief rabbi of Prague.
Courtesy Liselotte Ivry

"What happened exceeds our greatest dreams...I have been a witness to the magnificent, heroic fighting of Jewish men in battle."
—Mordechai Anielewicz, leader of the Warsaw Ghetto Uprising, in a letter written in 1943

Passover Facts

The March of the Living

Both Ben and Liselotte have gone on The March of the Living, an international Holocaust education program that brings teenagers to Auschwitz-Birkenau concentration camp to learn about the Holocaust.

Since 1988, more than 200,000 teenagers from thirty-five countries have taken part.

Holocaust educators, spiritual leaders and Holocaust survivors accompany the teens. Participants march 3 kilometers (1.8 miles) from Auschwitz to Birkenau.

Liselotte has gone on the march three times. "It was not an easy thing to visit the places where I was," she says. But Liselotte is committed to Holocaust education. "It's important to teach young people about the things we witnessed," she said.

the morning because my uncle explained all the passages in the Haggadah. I remember I felt very good there. For all of us Jews, it was a celebration of freedom after going through the horrors of the Second World War," she says.

In 1949, Liselotte moved to Canada, where another uncle had settled. At work in Montreal at an importing company, she met her future husband, Sidney Ivry. Sidney was one of six children, and soon Liselotte was celebrating Passover with the Ivry clan. "When Sidney's sister invited me to her seder, I remember that I bought a beautiful blue suit at Morgan's Department Store. The suit was very snazzy. But that seder was bittersweet for me. I had lost all my family. But life had to go on. I had to keep living," Liselotte says.

Liselotte and Sidney married in 1950. After they had children, the couple made the seder at their home. Once the children were in school, Liselotte studied to become an art teacher for preschoolers. Later, she earned a bachelor's degree.

Liselotte has two grown children, five grandchildren and five great-grandchildren. In her free time, she knits squares that are sewn together to make quilts for women seeking refuge at a shelter for battered Jewish women. "But I don't knit on **Shabbat**," Liselotte says, "to honor my mother."

Liselotte calls Passover "the festival of freedom." It is the Jewish holiday that means most to her. "From way back, Jews always had to find a way to survive. We were survivors from Day One," she says.

Despite all she has endured, Liselotte still believes in God. "There must be something," she tells me on a fall day, pointing to a bare tree outside. "If we look at trees without one leaf left, they look completely dead. And then comes spring and it all starts over again. Some people call it nature. I call it God."

March of the Living.
Sam Churchill

The Warsaw Ghetto Uprising: 1943

One of the things the Nazis did after invading Poland in 1939 was confine Jews to sealed ghettos, parts of cities where only Jews could live. There, residents faced overcrowding, starvation and, because they were denied medical care, disease. There were some 27,000 apartments in the Warsaw ghetto. When Warsaw was declared a ghetto in 1940, it was common for six or seven people to have to share a room.

From the start, it was the young people in the ghetto who protested. The older people tried talking them out of it, fearing that by speaking up things might become even worse. In March 1941, 70,000 more Jews were brought to the ghetto, bringing the population to nearly half a million. Many died of starvation or disease.

There were also mass deportations. Those who were deported were sent to death camps such as Auschwitz. In the summer of 1942, some 250,000 Jews were deported from Warsaw to Treblinka, another death camp. When the Jews remaining in the ghetto heard rumors of the fate of those who were deported, they took action.

The Warsaw Ghetto Uprising was led by Mordechai Anielewicz, who was twenty-three. Anielewicz and his friends formed a group called ZOB, which stands for the Zydowska Organizacja Bojowa, Polish for Jewish Fighting Organization.

In January 1943, ZOB fighters, who had smuggled weapons into the ghetto, fired on Nazi troops—and the Nazis retreated.

The Haggadah continues to evolve. Some families add a reference in their Haggadah to the Holocaust. Here is an example of one such addition: As we were all slaves in Egypt, so tonight all of us are survivors of the Shoah.

Residents of the Warsaw Ghetto gather to celebrate Passover.
Yad Vashem

On April 18, 1943—the day before Passover—the **Gestapo** assured the Jewish elders in charge of the ghetto that its residents would remain safe. But a member of the Resistance learned the Nazis were planning an action for that very night. Ghetto residents prepared themselves with hand grenades, revolvers and homemade bombs.

On Passover, the Nazis charged into the ghetto. Resistance fighters drove the Nazis out. The next day, the Nazis returned with tanks.

The ZOB kept the Nazis at bay for nearly a month. The fighting ended on May 16, 1943, when the Nazis destroyed the Great Synagogue on Tlomacki Street. Historians believe Anielewicz died in the ghetto on May 8, 1943, when the Nazis broke into the bunker where he and his friends were hiding.

The Warsaw Ghetto Uprising is the best-known example of physical resistance during the Holocaust. The members of the ZOB may not have won, but their courageous effort reminds us to stand up against oppression and that even a small group of committed people can make a difference.

Jewish women bake matzo for Passover in the Warsaw ghetto.
Yad Vashem

"How wonderful that no one need wait a single moment to start to improve the world."
—*Anne Frank*

Recipe for Matzo Brittle

You Will Need:

6 sheets matzo
½ cup unsalted butter
1 cup brown sugar
½ teaspoon salt
½ teaspoon vanilla extract
1½ cups semi-sweet chocolate chips
1 cup chopped pecans

Instructions:

Break matzo into pieces and arrange on baking sheet. In a pan over low heat, mix butter, brown sugar and salt. Boil for five minutes, stirring occasionally. Remove from heat; stir in vanilla. Pour mixture over matzo. Bake at 175 degrees Celsius (350 degrees Fahrenheit) for ten minutes.

Remove from oven and sprinkle with chocolate chips. Wait five minutes, then spread the chocolate with a spatula. Sprinkle nuts on top. Refrigerate for fifteen minutes before serving.

THREE

PASSOVER IN ACTION

It is customary for the youngest child at the seder to ask the four questions.

Abbie Miller/Stories Framed Photography, LLC

Kids and Passover

Kids play an important role in the celebration of Passover. The youngest child at the seder table asks the four questions (p. 17) that help us tell the story of Passover.

It is also the children who search for the afikomen. This ancient game of hide-and-seek is not only part of the seder ritual, it is also a way for kids to have fun. The Passover story deals with difficult subjects such as slavery and oppression, but it also shows us that even in the most challenging times, laughter and joy are still possible.

Passover and the Obligation to Do Good

One of the first things that happens at the seder is that those gathered at the table give thanks for all their blessings. Once that is done, they join together to say, "We invite the less fortunate to share with us at this meal, and also at other times."

This obligation to share, to do good, and to give what is called in Hebrew **tzedakah** is an essential part of Passover, and an essential part of Jewish tradition in general. And it is not only grownups who can become **tzaddikim**, (Hebrew for "good people"); kids can too.

Looking after those who are less fortunate than we are is a way to assert our humanity. Of course, it is also a good way to distract us from our own troubles. When Liselotte Ivry was fifteen and living in Prague after the Nazis took over her hometown of Listany, she got into trouble with the uncle and aunt who were caring for her. Frustrated that their niece kept coming home past her curfew, they sent Liselotte to live at a residence for young people. It was while Liselotte was living in the residence that she began volunteering at a Jewish seniors' facility. Liselotte was one of about twenty teenaged volunteers who delivered lunches to the residents. "It was a good experience. The seniors were happy to see a young face," Liselotte recalls.

Why is it that some people are inclined to do good? Social scientists who have studied the roots of **altruism**—a concern for the welfare of others—believe that altruism is often learned in a family, community or culture. So it is not surprising that children raised by altruistic parents often turn out to be altruistic. Liselotte credits her mother for teaching her about tzedakah. "My mother instilled in

Giving thanks before the seder meal.
LoloStock/Shutterstock.com

Every week, religious Jews observe a day of rest known as the Sabbath (or Shabbat). From sunset on Friday until sunset on Saturday, they do not drive, make phone calls or even write. However, the preservation of human life overrides even the laws of Shabbat.

Passover Facts

The Tzedakah Box

Before the Sabbath and Holy Days such as Passover, it is customary for Jewish children to drop money for charity into a tzedakah box. In the early 1900s, blue and white tin tzedakah boxes became popular in Canada, the United States and Europe. These boxes were issued by the Jewish National Fund, an organization that sought to raise money to help purchase land in Palestine for a Jewish state. That dream was realized when the State of Israel was established in 1948.

This silver tzedakah, or charity box, comes from Charleston, South Carolina, and dates back to 1820. It is now part of the collection at the National Museum of American Jewish History in Philadelphia.
Wikipedia

us the importance of being kind to others—not only by giving money," Liselotte says.

When Liselotte's children were enrolled in a Jewish day school in Montreal, she always gave them a little extra money on Friday—for the school's tzedakah box. "It's a Jewish tradition to do tzedakah. It teaches young people to share," says Liselotte.

Although Liselotte is growing old and has faced some serious health issues, she continues to do tzedakah. In 2008, she learned that the very same Jewish seniors' residence in Prague where she had volunteered as a teenager needed extensive renovations. Liselotte went into action—she contributed money of her own and asked friends for donations. She explained that many of the seniors living in the residence were, like her, Holocaust survivors. "I told my friends, 'These people need to be looked after,'" Liselotte says. And it worked—Liselotte and her friends managed to raise $50,000 for the seniors' residence, and Liselotte traveled to Prague to present the cheque.

At Passover, it is considered an act of tzedakah to invite people who are alone during the Holy Days to your seder. After Liselotte's father's death, the neighbors who invited Liselotte, her brother and their mother to their seder were tzaddikim.

Montreal Food Baskets

Montrealer Sylvia Lerman always makes the second Passover seder at her home in Dollard-des-Ormeaux, on Montreal's West Island. Nine people gather around Sylvia's dining room table: her husband, Brian, their parents, as well as the couple's twin sons, Michael and Sean. But it wouldn't be a seder without Sylvia's neighbor, Danielle, who is also Jewish and whose family lives in the United States.

Since she was 11 years old, Sylvia, who is in her late forties, has been involved in a special Passover project that embodies tzedakah. Montreal Food Baskets was established in 1947 and is run entirely by volunteers.

Back in 1977, Sylvia joined the youth division of the local B'nai Brith—an international Jewish service organization—and all the members of her chapter had to help prepare Passover food baskets for the needy. "I went because I had to go—but I never stopped going since then," says Sylvia.

When Sylvia married Brian in 1990, she got him involved in Montreal Food Baskets too. As for the twins, they can hardly remember a Passover when they did not

"The text of the Haggadah is the same whether it's in Hebrew and English, or Hebrew and Italian, or Hebrew and Spanish. But depending where we live and who we are, we make changes."
—Nira Friedman, Montreal-based Hebrew teacher who was raised on a **kibbutz** in Israel

The twins, helping to stock Passover baskets when they were younger. Michael is holding the honey cake. Sean is hanging on to the shopping cart.
Courtesy Sylvia Lerman

volunteer to help prepare, and later to deliver, the food baskets. "When we were really little, they'd set up the boxes on a table and we'd walk on the table and drop food into the boxes," recalls Sean.

In its early years, Montreal Food Baskets, which was founded by a chapter of B'nai Brith, delivered about 100 food baskets annually—half at **Rosh Hashanah**, the Jewish New Year, and half at Passover. Today, Montreal Food Baskets prepares a whopping 4,000 baskets every year!

Sheldon Popliger has volunteered with the organization for more than thirty-five years. He believes that most people are unaware of the level of poverty that exists in major cities such as Montreal. "Once I knocked on a door and a man said, 'Come in.' He was in a wheelchair and the only furniture he had was a mattress and a TV on a plastic TV table. Another time, I delivered a basket to a family that was living in a basement locker. They had to use the toilet in the building's garage," says Sheldon.

> "Passover is a way for parents to pass on Jewish traditions, memories and values to their children."
> —Rabbi Elina Bykova, a Montreal resident born and raised in Kiev, Ukraine, where Jews were forbidden to practice their religion

Preparing baskets for Passover 2014. It's hard work, but that doesn't mean there is no time to play.
Courtesy Sylvia Lerman

Individuals and families who want to receive a Passover basket apply through various Montreal Jewish social service agencies. The names of the people who receive Passover baskets are never revealed. That is because treating those who are less fortunate than us with respect is another Jewish tradition.

Though the organization is called Montreal Food Baskets, the baskets are actually cardboard boxes. At Passover, each box includes some twenty-five items, all **kosher for Passover**. These items include matzo, a honey cake, as well as a chicken that is ready for roasting or to turn into chicken soup.

Many of the Passover basket recipients are seniors living on fixed incomes. Passover can be an expensive time of year for them, especially if they are observant Jews. "At Passover, there's a complete changeover of all the food in Jewish homes. Our baskets help out a lot of the families who couldn't afford to do that," says David Guttman, a Montreal businessman who helps coordinate Montreal Food Baskets and who also happens to be Sylvia's dad.

The volunteers who run Montreal Food Baskets work on the project year-round. But the real work begins around the second week of March when the organization opens its warehouse.

The biggest days, when the most volunteers are needed, are the two Sundays before Passover. This is when people come to collect their baskets. If the recipients have difficulty walking or taking public transport, volunteers deliver the baskets.

The twins never gripe about having to spend two Sundays helping out with Passover baskets. "I always look

Passover Facts

What Does Kosher for Passover Mean?

Kosher foods are foods that conform to Jewish dietary laws, called kashrut. These laws are set out in the Old Testament in the Books of Leviticus and Deuteronomy. For instance, it is not kosher to consume meat and milk at the same time. Neither shellfish nor pork are permitted.

Kosher for Passover means not having or eating any foods that are *chametz*—contain wheat, barley, rye, spelt, oats or any foods derived from these products.

Kosher for Passover foods are made with special Passover flour. Usually, these foods are produced under the supervision of a rabbi.

Label on bottle of orange juice certifying that is kosher for Passover. *Wikipedia*

Food boxes.
ArtisticCaptures/iStock.com

forward to it. It's fun. We get to hang out with friends and family—and help people," says Sean.

Despite the hard work, there is still time for fun. "Sometimes we jump around in the boxes," says Sean.

Now that they are older (and stronger), the twins get to help out with deliveries. Many of the people to whom the boys deliver boxes are elderly and live in seniors' residences. Others live in Montreal's poorer neighborhoods. Some are recent immigrants to Montreal, many from Russia. Sometimes, Michael and Sean are invited inside the people's apartments. "They don't have giant flat-screen TVs," says Michael. "They have what they need," Sean adds.

Though recipients of the Passover baskets are on tight budgets, it is not uncommon for them to insist on tipping the twins. But the boys never keep the tip money. Instead, it all goes right back to Montreal Food Baskets.

There are some tips the boys do get to keep—the non-monetary kind. "I've gotten chocolate bars," says Sean. "I keep those."

Over the years, the twins have brought friends to help with the Passover baskets. In 2011 and 2012, Sean, who is active in Scouts Canada, brought members of his troop (and even some of their family members) to help pack boxes. "Not all of them were Jewish," Sean explains.

The twins share a deep commitment to tzedakah. "We're always going to do it—" says Michael. Sean finishes his brother's sentence: "It's how we were brought up."

In Hebrew each letter of the alphabet has a numerical value. The word chai, meaning "life," has a numerical value of eighteen, which is considered to be a number representing good luck. Jews will often give gifts of money in multiples of eighteen, symbolically wishing life and/or luck to the recipient.

Passover Food Drive

Children also play an important part in Toronto's Passover Food Drive. Begun in 1983, the Passover Food Drive is organized by the National Council of Jewish Women of Canada, Toronto Section. In 2014, volunteers helped pack and deliver over 2,500 Passover food boxes for needy families living in the Toronto area. Glenda Ephron Cooper, chairperson of the drive, explained that much of the packing is done by young volunteers, most of whom attend local Jewish day schools or after-school Hebrew programs.

"Part of our school program involves the sale of matzo bricks," Glenda says. These bricks look like matzo, but are made of paper. Students buy the bricks, write their names

"Being Jewish is about much more than names and noses. It has to do with deep and diverse cultural traditions and heritages."
—*Rabbi Barbara Aiello, who works as a rabbi in both Calabria, Italy, and Sarasota, Florida*

A woman prepares packages of food to give to the poor for Passover in Ashdod, Israel, in 2011.
ChameleonsEye/Shutterstock.com

These drawings, produced by Toronto school children, were sold as greeting cards to raise money for Toronto's Passover Food Drive.
Courtesy Toronto Passover Food Drive

Young child with tzedakah box.
mocker_bat/iStock.com

on them, and then the bricks are displayed on a wall at their school.

In 2014, Glenda and her team needed to raise extra money to cover the cost of purchasing kosher chickens, which had previously been donated. When students heard about the situation, they came up with a plan: to sell paper chickens in addition to the matzo bricks.

That year, the organization also introduced a contest in which students at Jewish day schools were asked to draw a picture depicting what Passover means to them. The best five drawings were turned into greeting cards that were sold to raise additional funds for the drive.

Every Passover food box that is delivered by the organization comes with a personalized card, made by the child who packed the box. "This makes the recipient feel that the box is personal, that someone cares," says Glenda.

Kehila Jewish Community Day School

Even a small school can make a big difference.

In the 2014–2015 school year, only twenty-six students were enrolled at Kehila Jewish Community Day School (KJCDS) in Hamilton, Ontario. Every Friday is Tzedakah Friday at the small school. Students, whether they are in kindergarten or in the school's senior grade five class, can contribute money to the school's beautifully decorated tzedakah jar. "It's usually one of the older kids who goes around to each classroom with the jar," says Michele Schneider, office administrator at KJCDS.

Every month, the school chooses another charity to support. In March 2014, the tzedakah money went to the food bank associated with Jewish Social Services in nearby Dundas. "Every year, we also set a date to collect kosher for Passover food. The food we collect also goes to the food bank," says Michele.

But the tzedakah money does not go only to Jewish organizations. In 2012, following a devastating earthquake in the Philippines, KJCDS sent the money to the Red Cross.

Bram Ogus loves when it is his turn to go from classroom to classroom with the tzedakah jar. "It makes me feel like a superhero. When I have children, I will teach them that tzedakah is the greatest **mitzvah**, or good deed, to do at school. It is as important as learning a subject like Hebrew and English," Bram says.

On some Tzedakah Fridays at Kehila Jewish Community Day School, Bram Ogus goes from class to class collecting money for a variety of charities.
Courtesy Kehila School

The Friendship Circle

The Friendship Circle is a Montreal-based Jewish organization that provides social programs for children and teens with special needs. Here, young people—not all of them Jewish—with conditions such as autism spectrum disorder (ASD), Down syndrome, attention deficit disorder (ADD), and attention deficit hyperactivity disorder (ADHD) take part in activities and develop their social skills.

All kids, even those who are differently abled, can do tzedakah. "We teach the kids who come here that they are not alone, that they are an active and integral part of our community, and that they can help others," says Rabbi Leibele Rodal, program director of the Friendship Circle.

In preparation for Passover, children at the Friendship Circle make afikoman bags and decorated **Haggadot**.

"I would say to young people... remember that there is meaning beyond absurdity. Let them be sure that every little deed counts, that every word has power."
—*Rabbi Abraham Joshua Heschel*

Unlike Passover, Hanukkah, a Jewish holiday celebrated in December, is not mentioned in the Bible. Hanukkah is believed to have originated in the mid-nineteenth century.

In 2014, the children delivered these items to local Jewish eldercare facilities. "We wanted to bring the joy of the holiday to others. Many of the elderly we visited do not live with their families. We told them, 'We are your family and we are here to celebrate Passover with you,'" says Rabbi Rodal.

For Rabbi Rodal, Passover is about crossing boundaries—which is what the Israelites did when they escaped slavery. "We must go beyond our limitations every day. That's an especially important lesson for kids with special needs," he says.

King David High School

Melanie Kunista and a volunteer show off the afikoman bag Melanie made at the Friendship Circle.
The Friendship Circle

"It is not enough to learn about tzedakah. If that learning doesn't transform into action, it is empty learning," says Rabbi Stephen Berger, who teaches Jewish studies at King David High School in Vancouver, British Columbia.

Doing tzedakah is part of the curriculum all year round at this Vancouver high school. Every week, students sign up to visit the elderly at a local Jewish seniors' residence or to volunteer at The Door Is Open, a drop-in center for the homeless on Vancouver's East Side.

Because the school is closed at Passover, the students make some extra trips to the seniors' residence before the holiday. "They sing to the residents as a way to get them in the holiday spirit," says Rabbi Berger.

Rabbi Berger also asks his students to write commentary on the Passover story and to include it in their own personalized Hagaddot. He encourages them to relate the Passover story to issues that are relevant to them, such as freedom and environmental disasters. Berger's students put on sleep masks so they can better understand the concept of darkness. They also contemplate loss and hunger. "I've had students write about freedom from cell phones and how vegetarians relate to the use of the shank bone on the seder plate. It's important for teens to feel Passover is real to them," Rabbi Berger says.

In 2010, Rabbi Berger accompanied a Jewish youth group to New York, where they saw matzo being made. That inspired Rabbi Berger's latest plan: to buy a portable propane brick oven so that students can make their own matzo. "If things work out, I'm hoping that by Passover of 2015, each child will have matzo for their own seder. Then we'll deliver all the extra matzo to local Jewish families in need," he says.

Members of the Friendship Circle deliver matzo to a seniors' residence. From left to right, Zali Rodal, Rabbi Rodal, Joshua Benlolo and volunteer Brian Lankin.
The Friendship Circle

Recipe for Chicken Soup

You Will Need:

3-pound chicken, cut into pieces

2 celery stalks, diced

2 carrots, sliced

1 parsnip, sliced

1 onion, cut into chunks

1 turnip, cut into chunks

¼ cup dill

Chicken soup.
Wikipedia

Instructions:

Place chicken in large pot, cover with water and bring to boil. Skim off the grease. Add remaining ingredients. Cover and simmer for ninety minutes.

FOUR

Passover Around the World

The Passover story and the emphasis on telling it in a certain order is a way of bringing together Jews from around the world and across time. And yet because every family is unique, we create our own Passover traditions.

When they first got married, my friends Deena and Terry Creatchman, who lived in Montreal at the time, noticed a typographical error in the English section of their Haggadah. The error occurred during a story about the pharaoh. Instead of reading, "Pharaoh decreed only against the males," their Haggadah (which, by the way, was the same version used by most North American Jewish families at the time) read, "Pharaoh decreed only against the *the* males." Because Deena and Terry like to laugh and

Deena and Terry Creatchman with their sons, Carl (left) and Eric (right). For this family, laughter is part of the seder.

Courtesy Deena Sacks Creatchman

share an interest in grammar, they decided to make the extra *the* part of their Passover celebration.

The couple's two sons, Eric and Carl, were raised with the tradition. "It's our way of telling who is concentrating and listening. If they [the boys] don't correct the extra 'the,' we know they aren't paying attention," says Deena, who now lives in Hamilton, Ontario. In fact, in 2014, when the Creatchmans attended a seder at the home of cousins who use a newer—and more grammatically correct—version of the Haggadah, the Creatchmans missed the extra *the*. "It wasn't the same without it," says Deena.

It isn't only families who find ways to make Passover their own. Countries do it too. Put on your seatbelt! This chapter is about to take you on whirlwind trip to Passover seders around the world.

Israel

Israel is the only country in the world where Passover lasts seven days, instead of eight. That is because in Exodus 12:14, Jews are commanded: *for seven days you are to eat bread without yeast*. The extra day was added so **diaspora Jews**—Jews living in countries outside of Israel—would not miss the official start of Passover because they lived in another time zone.

In Israel, Passover is one of three **pilgrimage** holidays. That means Jews from across the country, as well as tourists who make the trip to Israel for the holiday, go to pray at Jerusalem's Western Wall. For many years, the Western Wall was known as the Wailing Wall. Israelis use the Hebrew word **kotel**, which means "wall," to refer to the

Man praying at the Western Wall—notice the notes left in the wall.
Wikipedia

The ancestors of Ashkenazi Jews came from France, Germany and eastern Europe.

Western Wall. For Jews, the kotel, which is all that remains of the ancient First and Second Temples, is considered the holiest spot on Earth.

"You can't go to Jerusalem without touching the wall and leaving a note," says Nira Friedman, who was raised on a kibbutz, or communal settlement in Israel, but who has lived in Montreal since 1961. "The notes say things like, *Please heal someone who is sick* or *Let me pass my exam*," says Nira.

For thirty years, Nira taught Hebrew to grade one students at Jewish People's and Peretz Schools (JPPS) in Montreal. These days, Nira, who is 82, continues to teach Hebrew to private students. One of those students is my niece Claudia Lighter.

Nira spends part of every year in Israel, where she always goes to Ramat Yochanan, the kibbutz near Haifa where she was born and raised and which she still considers home. In Israel, there is only one seder, celebrated on the first night of Passover. At Ramat Yochanan, all 800 residents attend a giant communal seder. "The community becomes a family," Nira explains.

In Israel, like everywhere else, Passover represents freedom. But Nira says in her homeland, Passover is also a way to celebrate the arrival of spring. "If there was a lot of rain in winter—that's something we want—then we have wheat and barley to harvest," she explains. According to Jewish law, Israeli Jews must wait thirty-three days after Passover before they can start harvesting grain from the wheat family.

Over the years, the **kibbutzniks** (residents of a kibbutz) at Ramat Yochanan have transformed the Haggadah. "We add commentary. We add material about the Holocaust and the Israeli army. Where the traditional Haggadah mentions four sons, we welcome all the new babies by name who were born on the kibbutz," Nira explains. "In this way, the Haggadah is alive and organic," she adds.

The Netherlands

The Dutch are known for their tulips, their windmills and the pleasure they take in cleaning! When I was a child, my Dutch mother used to walk around the house with a washcloth in one hand—just in case she found a spot of dirt! Perhaps this attitude helps explain why many Dutch Jews associate Passover with spring cleaning, the **grote schoonmaak**.

It is believed the first Jews arrived in the Netherlands in the eleventh century. Even then, the country was known for its openness.

Passover Facts

Ever Wonder Why Matzos Have All Those Little Holes?

Matzos have holes because in ancient times, matzos were stamped with beautiful designs. But rabbis worried that this practice took too much time and that the wheat might leaven and rise. So they decided that the only design could be straight rows of holes. Nowadays, those holes come in handy: rabbis inspect matzo by breaking it along the holes, and then against the grain in order to ensure that the matzo is cooked through and unleavened.

Seder at Kibbutz Ramat Yochanan in the 1930s. Nira is the second girl from the left in the top row, looking away from the camera.
courtesy Nira Friedman

In 1878, my great-great-grandfather Jozef L. Spier laid the first stone for the synagogue in Zutphen, a historic city in the center of the Netherlands. But with time, my family became less observant. My mother's only childhood memories of Passover have to do with eating matzo, which my grandmother slathered with sweet butter and then sprinkled with sugar.

Another Dutch Passover delicacy is **gremchelich**—pancakes made from matzo, and usually served for dessert.

China

In 2014, for the first time in over 150 years, a Passover seder was held in China. Located in China's Hunan province, the city of Kaifeng is home to an estimated 500 to 1,000 Jews. Kaifeng's Jewish community is nearly 1,000 years old. Between the fourteenth and seventeenth centuries, some 5,000 Jews lived in Kaifeng, but the number dropped because of **assimilation** and intermarriage.

Nepal

Believe it or not, the world's biggest seder is held in Kathmandu, the capital city of Nepal! Known as *The Seder on Top of the World*, this seder was first celebrated in 1989 by Jewish trekkers traveling through Nepal. That year, they joined together for a seder meal at the Pumpernickel Bakery in Thamel, a section of Kathmandu that is popular with tourists.

The first female rabbi was Regina Jonas. She was ordained in East Berlin in 1935.

The stone laid in 1878 by my great-great-grandfather Jozef L. Spier at the synagogue in Zutphen, the Netherlands.
Nationale Beeldbank

RESTAURATIE 1985
DE EERSTE STEEN
HERPLAATST DOOR
MEIJER GROEN
DEN 24^{E} ELLOEL / 10 SEPTEMBER 5745

DE EERSTE STEEN GELEGD
DOOR
JOZEF. L. SPIER.
DEN 16^{E} TAMMOEZ / 11 JULIJ 5638

Since then, The Seder on Top of the World has grown—and grown. These days, the seder is held in a hotel. In 2012, over a thousand guests attended the seder. With so many people, preparations begin months in advance. Eleven hundred pounds of matzo were transported by ship from Israel to India, and then trucked to Nepal.

Many of those who take part in The Seder on Top of the World are young Israeli backpackers who have recently completed their service in the Israeli army.

In 2014, Amit Asher Shapira, 28, attended The Seder on Top of the World. Amit, who comes from Ramat Yishai, in Israel, is a student at a **Buddhist** monastery in Nepal. "I'm a Buddhist and a proud Jew as well," he said. Amit enjoyed the singing and dancing at The Seder on Top of the World. "Even the Nepalese waiters were wearing kippahs. Passover reminds us where we came from. That's the only way we can know where we are going to," he said.

Italy

Italian Jews hold their seder on the fifth night of Passover. This tradition, known as *seder hamishi* (*hamishi* is the Yiddish word for "cozy") dates back to the early sixteenth century, following the Inquisition, when many Jews in countries such as Italy, Spain and Portugal were forced to convert to Christianity, and those who refused to do so could practice their religion only in secret.

Delaying the seder until the fifth night was a way to avoid the authorities' suspicion. Sometimes, non-Jewish neighbors showed their support by allowing their Jewish friends to conduct their seders in their *cantinas*, or basements.

Passover Facts

That's a Matzo Boulder—Not a Ball!

According to *The Guinness Book of World Records*, the world's largest matzo ball was unveiled in Tucson, Arizona, in 2010 at the Tucson Jewish Food Festival. To make his 488-pound matzo ball, Chef Jon Wirtis used 125 pounds of matzo meal, 25 pounds of chicken fat, 20 pounds of potato starch and more than 1,000 eggs. In case you are wondering, the pot Chef Wirtis used for cooking his giant matzo ball was 6 feet high and 6 feet wide.

"And you shall love the other person as yourself."
—Leviticus 19:18

Kosher rice.
Wikipedia

A former puppeteer, Rabbi Barbara Aiello divides her time between southern Italy and Sarasota, Florida. Since 2004, she has been the rabbi in Serrastretta, Italy. Every Passover, Rabbi Aiello and members of her congregation walk twenty-three kilometers (fourteen miles) to Lamezia Terme (formerly called Nicastro), the location of what was once Calabria's thriving Jewish quarter.

In Italy, the local rice is considered kosher for Passover, "Though it has to be sifted through to ensure there is nothing else in it," says Rabbi Aiello. Don't look for a white egg on the Italian seder plate. Their egg, which is slow cooked for five hours in a mixture of water and saffron, is brown—inside and out.

At an Italian seder, both the matzo and the seder plate are passed from head to head. This gesture is meant to recall the

The egg on the Italian seder plate is brown inside and out because it is slow-cooked in water and saffron.
Blueenayim/Dreamstime.com

heavy burden of slavery. If the plate is too heavy for a child, the woman of the house holds it over the child's head instead.

"Passover has a special meaning for us. Our struggle continues in that often we are not recognized as authentic Jews. So we are fighting for our freedom—not from outside oppression, but from within the established Jewish community, as we strive to be fully recognized as Jews," says Rabbi Aiello.

Ukraine

When Rabbi Elina Bykova was growing up in Kiev, Ukraine, she knew little about Passover. That is because under the Communist regime, all religions were banned. The government insisted that everyone in the Union of Soviet Socialist Republics (USSR), of which Ukraine was a founding member, had to be atheist, meaning they did not believe in God's existence. "I only knew that I liked matzo," says Rabbi Bykova, who now lives in Montreal, where she works as a freelance rabbi.

When she was a child growing up in Ukraine in the 1960s and 1970s, Rabbi Bykova and her family could not practice Judaism. "People who had jobs could get fired if it was discovered they went to synagogue, and students could lose their spots in school," Rabbi Bykova explains. Only her grandfather, who was retired, could risk going to the synagogue in Kiev to buy matzo. "We had it with scrambled eggs. All my non-Jewish friends loved it too," Rabbi Bykova recalls.

It was only after **Perestroika** (restructuring of the Soviet political and economic system), and **Glasnost** (which means "openness"), that Soviet Jews like Rabbi Bykova

At the seder hamishi in Italy, Alessandro Amato holds the plate of matzo over the head of his mom, Angela Yael Amato.
Domenico Pulice

The oldest Haggadah is more than 1,000 years old. It was found in Old Cairo, Egypt.

Ethiopian women at the Western Wall during the week of Passover.
Wikipedia

Falasha woman prepares a meal.
Wikipedia

and her family could rediscover their Jewish roots. Rabbi Bykova began to learn about Passover in 1990, when rabbis came to Ukraine to help educate its Jewish population. Then in 1991, Rabbi Bykova went to London, England, to train as a rabbi at Leo Baeck College.

"For me, Passover is about freedom. Today, Ukraine is fighting for its freedom. It makes me think how precious freedom is. Even in democratic societies, we are enslaved by so many things. We are slaves of money and jobs. Passover makes us ask ourselves, 'What is real?' 'What is important?'" says Rabbi Bykova.

Ethiopia

The **Falasha** are Jews who migrated to Ethiopia after the destruction of the First Temple by the Babylonians in 586 BCE. But in Ethiopia the Falasha faced terrible persecution. Even the term *Falasha*, which dates back to the

fifteenth century, is considered derogatory because it means "foreigner" or "exile."

In 1977, concerned about the mistreatment of the Falasha, Israel began airlifting Falasha from Ethiopia so they could begin new lives in Israel.

Today, most Falasha live in Israel, though some have made homes in other countries such as Canada. When the Falasha gather to celebrate Passover, they incorporate some of the Passover customs from Ethiopia. One of these customs is the breaking of the family's earthenware dishes. This custom symbolizes a break from the past and a new beginning. Falasha-style matzo is often made with chickpea flour. Because the Falasha had no Hagaddot, it is customary for them to read directly from the biblical story of Exodus. And because the Falasha are known for their colorful handicrafts, Falasha seder tables are often decorated with homemade tablecloths and matzo covers.

Iraq

Long ago, Baghdad, the capital city of Iraq, was home to a vibrant Jewish community. Jewish exiles first arrived in the country, which was then known as Babylon, in 597 BCE. Some stayed for sixty years—until they were permitted to return to Jerusalem. Others chose to remain in Baghdad. In 1917, during the British occupation of Iraq, about one-third of Baghdad's population was Jewish.

But over the years, life became increasingly difficult for Jewish Iraqis, who faced terrible **anti-Semitism** (hatred of Jews). Most moved to Israel. Some settled in Canada and the United States. Today there are virtually no Jews left in Baghdad.

Passover Facts

The Real Story of the Orange on the Seder Plate

I was sitting at Nira Friedman's dining room table when she told me the story of the orange on the seder plate.

"About ten years ago, in New York, a woman in a Conservative synagogue read from the bimah (the podium where the Torah, sacred Jewish writings, is read), and a rabbi called out, 'A woman on the bimah is like an orange on the seder plate.'" And so now, every Passover, we add an orange to the seder plate."

I decided to do a little research—and tracked down the woman behind the story! Susannah Heschel is a professor of Jewish Studies at Dartmouth College in New Hampshire. As it turns out, the real story of the orange on the seder plate is a little more complicated than the version most people tell.

The real story dates back to the mid-1980s, when Susannah was visiting Oberlin College in Ohio and was shown a Haggadah written by students who wanted to add a feminist perspective. Their Haggadah included a story about a girl who

Continued on page 60 ♦ ♦ ♦

Passover Facts

♦ ♦ ♦ *Continued from page 59*

asks a rabbi whether lesbians have a place in Judaism. Angered by the question, the rabbi answers, "There's as much room for a lesbian in Judaism as there is for a crust of bread on the seder plate."

Susannah knew if she put a crust of bread on the seder plate, it would be a violation of Passover because of the rules against having leavened bread in the house. So at the next Passover, Susannah decided to add an orange to her family's seder plate. "I chose an orange because it suggests the fruitfulness for all Jews when lesbians and gay men are contributing and active members of Jewish life," she says.

Susannah never expected her gesture to catch on with Jewish families around the world. "I don't know how to account for the rapid and broad spread of the orange custom. I'm constantly amazed to hear from people overseas that they are placing an orange on the seder plate and talking about issues of homophobia, marginalization within the Jewish community, and so forth. I'm very glad the custom has become a stimulus for self-reflection," she says.

Yet, no matter where they now live, many Jews of Iraqi descent continue to celebrate Passover the way their ancestors did in Baghdad. Iraqi Jews substitute lemon juice for salt water. The charoset on their seder plates is a thick date paste or syrup called **halek**. And Iraqi Jews skip the traditional matzo ball soup. Instead, like Jews in Italy, they eat rice—only they serve theirs with meat kebabs.

What is perhaps most interesting about an Iraqi-style seder is that children do not ask the four questions as a way of retelling the Passover story. Instead, Iraqi Jewish children re-enact the story of the Exodus from Egypt. This custom is also popular with other **Sephardic Jews**—Jews who come from Spain, Portugal, North Africa and other parts of the Middle East. At an Iraqi-style seder, a child will ask, usually in either Arabic or Hebrew, "Where have you come from?" and another child answers, "From Egypt." "Where are you going?" the first child asks. The answer is, of course, "To Jerusalem."

Iraqi and other Sephardic Jews believe that by acting out the story of the Exodus, children—and the adults who watch their performance—will gain a more deeply felt understanding of what it means to escape slavery.

Morocco

It seems fitting to end this trip around the world in Morocco. That is because what sets the Moroccan Passover apart is the festive celebration called **Noce de Mimouna** that follows it. But Noce de Mimouna is more than a party with yummy things to eat. It also symbolizes the friendship and goodwill that exists between Jews and non-Jews.

Noce de Mimouna marks the end of Passover. Some people think the festivity, which takes place on the night after Passover, was named for Rabbi Yosef Maimon, the Moroccan-born father of the famous Jewish doctor and philosopher Maimonides.

Others believe the term is connected to the Arabic word for *wealth* or *good luck*.

Long ago, on the night after Passover ended, non-Jews in Morocco used to bring trays loaded with **mufleta**—traditional Moroccan pancakes—to their Jewish neighbors. The mufleta were a way to help Jews re-introduce chametz, or leavened foods, into their diet.

Nowadays, many Jewish families in Morocco, as well as Moroccan Jews who have settled in other countries such as Israel, Canada and the United States, make their own

Susannah Heschel, the woman who came up with the idea of the orange on the Passover plate.
Courtesy Susannah Heschel

Shani, a student at Akiba-Schechter Jewish Day School in Chicago, Illinois, celebrates Noce de Mimouna by baking the traditional pancake bread with Tamav, a young Israeli woman.
Copyright Akiba-Schechter Jewish Day School

Noce de Mimouna. The table is laid with symbolic foods. There is fish for good luck. Dates symbolize righteousness. Eggs and greens represent fertility. Cookies made with almonds and other nuts stand for joy and abundance. Flour, milk and honey are meant to remind the guests of Israel and purity.

Superstition has always played an important role in Moroccan culture. That is why you will often see the **hamsa** amulet, a decorative open hand with an eye in the middle, on the Noce de Mimouna table—it is supposed to ward off evil spirits. For Moroccan Jews, five is a special number. It is believed to serve as a reminder that we must praise God with all five of our senses. That explains why some Moroccan families display five pieces of gold jewelry on the Noce de Mimouna table. Others arrange five beans on a leaf or on pastry.

It is customary to leave the door to the house open on Noce de Mimouna. This tradition ensures that all are welcome—no matter their religion.

Recipe for Matzo Pancakes (Dutch Gremchelich)

You Will Need:

6 matzos, crumbled
Hot water
3 eggs
⅔ cup white sugar
¼ teaspoon cinnamon
½ cup raisins (soaked in water)
½ cup slivered almonds
Grated rind of ½ lemon
Oil for frying
Powdered sugar

Instructions:

Pour hot water over the crumbled matzos, then drain off the water. Beat eggs with sugar and cinnamon. Combine matzos and egg mixture. Pat raisins dry and add to batter along with almonds and lemon rind. Drop two tablespoons of mixture onto an oiled skillet. Turn with a spatula when golden brown. Serve with a dusting of powdered sugar.

Pancakes from matzo.
Yosefer/Dreamstime.com

Glossary

afikoman—half of a piece of matzo, hidden during the seder meal for children to search for before dessert

altruism—an unselfish concern for the welfare of others

anti-Semitism—hatred of Jews

assimilation—the process of fully adopting the ways of another culture

bar mitzvah (Hebrew for "son of the commandments")—a Jewish boy when he turns 13, meaning he is old enough to participate in all areas of Jewish life

bat mitzvah (Hebrew for "daughter of the commandments")—a Jewish girl when she turns 12, meaning she is old enough to participate in all areas of Jewish life

Buddhism—a religion of eastern and central Asia growing out of the teaching of Gautama Buddha

chametz—foods containing wheat, barley, rye, spelt, oats or any foods derived from these products

charoset—a sweet paste made from fruit and nuts used during the seder meal, symbolizing the mortar Jews used to make bricks when they were slaves in Egypt

Christianity—a monotheistic religion based on the teachings of Jesus Christ

concentration camp—a type of prison where large numbers of people who are not soldiers are kept during a war and are usually forced to live in very bad conditions

Dayenu (Hebrew for "we are grateful")—a song in which Jews thank God for his loving kindness and for performing miracles during their journey to the promised land

diaspora Jews—Jews living in countries outside of Israel

Erev Purim—the night before Purim, a Jewish holiday that commemorates the saving of the Jewish people from a conspiracy to destroy them

Falasha (Amharic for "foreigner")—a derogatory name for Jews who migrated to Ethiopia after the destruction of the First Temple by the Babylonians in 586 BCE

Gestapo—secret police of Nazi Germany

Glasnost (Russian for "openness")—a Soviet policy permitting open discussion of political and social issues and freer dissemination of news and information

gremchelich (Dutch)—pancakes made from matzo, a dessert prepared by Dutch Jews for the seder meal

grote schoonmaak (Dutch for "big cleaning")—a Dutch Jewish tradition of spring cleaning for Passover

Haggadah (pl. Haggadot; Hebrew for "to tell")—a Jewish book that sets out the order of events during the seder meal

halek—a thick date paste or syrup used by Iraqi Jews for the charoset in the seder meal

hamsa (Arabic)—an amulet with an open hand with an eye in the middle meant to ward off evil spirits during the Moroccan Noce de Mimouna

Hanukkah—a Jewish holiday (also known as the Festival of Lights) celebrated in December to commemorate the rededication of the Holy Temple in Jerusalem

hazeret—one of two bitter herbs (often romaine lettuce) used during the seder meal, to remind Jews of the bitterness of slavery

Hebrew—an ancient language spoken by people from Israel

Holocaust—the mass slaughter of European civilians and especially Jews by the Nazis during World War II

Islam—a monotheistic religion that teaches there is only one God and that Muhammad is God's prophet; the religion of Muslims

Judaism—the monotheistic religion developed among the ancient Hebrews that stresses belief in God and faithfulness to the laws of the Torah

karpas—a green vegetable (usually parsley or celery) that has been dipped in salt water and is used during the seder meal, symbolizing the arrival of spring and reminding Jews to give thanks for the gifts received from the earth

kashrut—Jewish dietary laws

kibbutz—a communal settlement in Israel

kibbutzniks—people living on a kibbutz

Kiddush—a blessing or prayer that begins the seder meal, thanking God for holidays like Passover

kippah (Hebrew; *yarmulke* in Yiddish)—a skullcap worn by Jewish men at times of prayer

kitl—a white garment worn by Jewish men, especially by the person leading the seder meal

kosher (*kashrut* in Hebrew)—dietary laws followed by Jewish people on a daily basis

kosher for Passover—dietary laws followed by Jewish people that respect specific laws for the Passover celebrations

kotel (Hebrew for "wall")—the Western Wall in Jerusalem, also known as the Wailing Wall, considered the holiest spot on Earth by Jews

Mah Nishtanah (Hebrew for "the four questions")—part of the seder meal when the youngest child asks the four questions about the history of Passover

manna—in the Bible, the food miraculously provided for the Israelites in the wilderness during their flight from Egypt

maror—one of two bitter herbs (often horseradish or horseradish root) used during the seder meal to remind Jews of the bitterness of slavery

matzo—a cracker-like, thin bread eaten especially by Jewish people at Passover

matzo loksh—a noodle pudding traditionally made from matzo, eggs and goose fat

mitzvah (Hebrew for "commandment")—a good deed

monotheistic—belief in a single god, rather than many gods

mufleta—a Moroccan pancake that helps Jews re-introduce leavened foods back into their diet after Passover

Noce de Mimouna—a Moroccan celebration to mark the end of Passover

Passover (*Paschal* in Hebrew)—a special holiday celebrated in the spring to remind Jewish people of their emergence from slavery more than 3,000 years ago

payos—side curls worn by Orthodox Jewish men, following the biblical instruction not to shave the corners of one's head

Perestroika (Russian)—a restructuring of the Soviet political and economic system

pilgrimage—a journey to a holy place

promised land—a place or condition believed to promise final satisfaction or realization of hopes, considered by Jewish people to be modern-day Israel

Rosh Hashanah—Jewish New Year

seder (Hebrew for "order")—a special meal that marks the beginning of Passover

seder hamishi (*hamish* is Yiddish for "cozy")—a special seder meal celebrated by Italian Jews on the fifth night of Passover

Sephardic Jews—Jews who come from Spain, Portugal, North Africa and other parts of the Middle East

Shabbat—the Jewish day of rest

Shoah—the Holocaust

synagogue—a building that is used for Jewish religious services

Torah—sacred Jewish writings

tzedakah—a religious obligation to do what is right and to show charity toward others

tzaddikim (Hebrew for "good people")—a person who fulfills their duty of tzedakah

Urchatz (Hebrew for "washing of the hands")—a symbolic act of purification during the seder meal

Yachatz—part of the seder meal when the afikoman is hidden and a special prayer is said inviting those who are hungry to share the meal

Yiddish—a language based on German that is written in Hebrew characters, originally spoken by Jews of central and eastern Europe

REFERENCES AND RESOURCES

Chapter One

Books:

Fellner, Judith B. *In the Jewish Tradition: A Year of Food and Festivities*.
New York: Smithmark Publishers, 1995.

Hopkowitz, Rabbi Yaakov. *Pesach for the Very Young*. Translated from Hebrew
by S. Hertz. Illustrated by Dan Barlev. Alev to Tav, 2011.

Websites:

BBC. Religions: Judaism. www.bbc.co.uk/religion/religions/judaism/

About: Religion. The Passover (Pesach) Story.
www.judaism.about.com/od/holidays/a/The-Passover-Pesach-Story.htm

The United Synagogue of Conservative Judaism.
www.uscj.org/perekyomi/passover_guide.htm

Chapter Two

Books:

Raphael, Chaim. *A Feast of History: The Drama of Passover Through the Ages*.
London: Weidenfeld & Nicolson, 1972.

Websites:

A Simple Jew: A Seder in Auschwitz.
www.asimplejew.blogspot.com/2006/04/seder-in-auschwitz.html

United with Israel.
www.unitedwithisrael.org/the-secret-seder-in-a-nazi-concentration-camp/

Chapter Three

Books:

Oliner, Samuel P and Pearl M. *Altruistic Personality: Rescuers of Jews in Nazi Europe*.
New York: Simon and Schuster, 1992.

Websites:

The Friendship Circle. www.friendshipcircle.ca

Montreal Food Baskets. www.montrealfoodbaskets.org

The Door is Open. www.thedoorisopen.ca

Chapter Four

Books:

Lehman-Wilzig, Tami. *Passover Around the World*. Illustrated by Elizabeth Wolf.
Minneapolis: Kar-Ben Publishing, 2006.

Websites:

Beliefnet: Unique Passover Traditions.
www.beliefnet.com/Faiths/Judaism/2009/03/Unique-Passover-Traditions.aspx?p=3

Happy Passover: Passover in Italy.
www.happypassover.net/around-the-world/passover-in-italy.html

INDEX

Page numbers in **bold** indicate an image; there may also be text related to the same topic on that page

Abrams, Lauren, **9**, **18**
afikoman, **16**, 20, 38, 47, **48**
Aiello, Rabbi Barbara, 45, 56–57
Akiba-Schechter Jewish Day School, 61
Alma-Tadema, Sir Lawrence, painter, 12
altruism, 39, 48. *See also* tzedakah; volunteering
Amato, Alessandro and Angela Yael, **57**
Angel of Death, 12
Anielewicz, Mordechai, 33, 36, 37
anti-Semitism, 59
Arabic language, 60, 61
Ashkenazi Jews, 51
assimilation, 54
Auschwitz-Birkenau extermination camp, **25**, 26, **32**, 33, 34, **35**, 36

B'nai Brith, Jewish service organization, 41, 42
Babylon, 59
Babylonians, 58
Baghdad, Iraq, 59, 60
Bamberg displaced persons camp, 27
Bergen-Belsen concentration camp, 26, 33
Bergen-Belsen displaced persons camp, 26
Berger, Rabbi Stephen, 48–49
Bernstein, Rabbi Phillip S., 23
bitter herbs, 15, 17, 18: hazeret, 15, **22**; maror, 15, 19
blessings. *See* prayers
bread: baked, 12, 17; burning of, **13**, 14; "Feast of Unleavened Bread," 15; leavened, 12, 60; manna, 13, 18; pancake, **61**; unleavened, "without yeast," 10, 15, 22, 51. *See also* matzo
Buddhism, 55
burning bush, 12
Bykova, Rabbi Elina, 42, 57–58

chametz, leavened, 43, 61
charity, **40**, 46. *See also* sharing with less fortunate; tzedakah; volunteering

charoset, fruit paste, 15, 18, 19, **20**, **22**, 60
chicken, **7**, 43, 46, **49**, 55
China, 54
Christianity, 8, 55
clothing, Jewish, **5**, **6**, **8**, 19, **28**, 33, **51**, **52**, 55, **57**
Communist regime, 57
concentration camps, 8, 26, 29: Auschwitz-Birkenau, **25**, 26, **32**, 33, 34, **35**, 36; Bergen-Belsen, 26, 33; Dachau, 26; Gurs detention camp, 31; Kaufering, 26; Theresienstadt, 32; Tiefstack, 33; Treblinka, 36; Vaihingen, 26
Cooper, Glenda Ephron, 45
Côte Saint-Luc neighborhood, Montreal, 7, 28, 29
Creatchman, Deena and Terry, **50**–51
Crossing the Red Sea, painting, **13**
Czechoslovakia, 29
Czech Jews, 29, 32
Czech Republic: Listany, **29**, 30, 31; Pilsen, 29, 30, 31; Prague, 31, 33, 39, 40

Dachau concentration camp, 26
Dalai Lama, 20
"Dayenu," song, 18
Death of Pharoah's Firstborn, painting, **12**
deportation of Jews, 25, 32, 36
Diary of Anne Frank, The, memoir, 27
diaspora Jews, 51
dietary laws, 43. *See also* kosher
displaced persons (DP) camps, 26, 27
displacement of Jews, 23, 26, 27
Dollard-des-Ormeaux neighborhood, Montreal, 22, 24, 40
donations, 40, 46
Door Is Open, The, 48
doors, symbolism of, 20, **21**, 62
Dutch Jews, 53–54

eggs, **15**, 30, 55, **56**, 57, 62
Egypt, 11–12, 15, 16, 17, 18, 23, 36, 57, 60
Egyptian people, **11**, 12, 18

Elijah, prophet, 20, 21
Erev Pesach, **52**
Erev Purim, 32
Ethiopia, **58**–59
Exodus, 12, 60
faith, 12, 23, 24, 27, 28, 33, 34
Falasha Jews, **58**–59
"Feast of Unleavened Bread," 15
flour, 13, 26, 43, 59, 62
food: bitter herbs, 15, 17, 18; bread, 10, 12, **13**, 14, 15, 17, 22, 51; charoset, 15, 18, 19, **20**, **22**, 60; chicken, **7**, 43, 46, **49**, 55; eggs, **15**, 30, 55, **56**, 57, 62; fish, 62; for seder, **7**, 14–**15**, **22**, 24, **41**, 43, **44**, **45**, 47, **49**, **56**, 59, **61**; goose, 22, 30; gremchelich, 54, **62**; halek, 60; hazeret, 15, **22**; karpas, 15, 16; kebabs, 60; kosher, 7–8, 20, 29, 43, 46, **56**; lamb shank, 12, **15**, 18, 49, **56**; lemon juice, 60; manna, 13, 18; maror, 15, 19; mufleta pancakes, **61**; oranges, 59–60, **61**; recipes, **20**, 37, **49**, 62; symbolism of, 10, **15**, 18, 19, 24; traditional, **15**, **20**, 37, **49**, 60, **61**, **62**; wine, 10, 15, 16, 18, 19, 20, 26. *See also* matzo
food baskets, 40–44: preparation of, **41**, **42**
food drive, 44, 46: delivery, 43, 44, 46, **49**
food festival, 55
four questions, 16, 17, 28, **38**, 60
Four Sons, story, 16–17, 53
Frank, Anne, 27
freedom, 10, 11, 12, 17, 18, 19, 20, 23, 26, 34, 49, 53, 57, 58
Friedman, Nira, 41, **52**–53, 59
Friendship Circle, 47–**48**
fundraising, 40, 45–46, 47

gas chambers, 25, 32, 33
gay and lesbian rights, 60
generosity. *See also* sharing with less fortunate; tzedakah
Germany, 27, 51
Gestapo, 37
Gladman, Emmanuella and Sam, **11**

Glasnost, 57
God, 8, 11, 12, 13, 15, 16, 19, 20, 24, 27, 28, 33, 34, 57, 62. *See also* faith
goose, 22, 30
gratitude, 15, 16, 17, 18, **39**
Great Synagogue, Warsaw, 37
gremchelich, 54, **62**
grote schoonmaak, 53
Gurs detention camp, 31
Guttman, David, 43

Hagaddah, The, 14, **15**, 18, 19, 26, **28**, 31, 34, 36, 41, 47, 50, 51, 53, 57, 59
halek, date paste, 60
hamsa amulet, 62, **63**
Hanukkah, 48
hazeret, horseradish, 15, **22**. *See also* bitter herbs
head: covering, **5**, **6**, 19, **28**, 33, **52**, 55, **57**; holding the seder plate over, 56–**57**; payos, **8**, **13**, 14; shaving of, 14, 25, 26
head of the family, role of, 15, 16, 19, 33
Hebrew: alphabet, 44; classes in, 45, 47, 52; language, 7, 41, 44, 60; word meanings, 14, 15, 18, 19, 39, 44, 51
Heschel, Susannah, 59, **61**
Holocaust, 8, 24–28, 29–34, 36–37, 53: education programs, 34, **35**; memorial, 31; survivors, 9, 24, **27**, 29, 30, **31**, 34, 40
homophobia, 60
horseradish, 15, **22**
human rights, 11, 20, 39
Hungarian Jews, **25**

immigration to Canada, 22, 44
Inquisition, 55
Iraqi Jews, 59–60
Islam, 8
Israel, State of, 5, 11, 13, 40, **51**, **52**, 53, 59, 61, 62. *See also* promised land
Israeli army, 53, 55
Israeli Jews, **14**, **28**, **51**, **52**, 55
Israelites, 11–13, 16, 17–18, 48
Italy, 45, 55–**57**, 60
Ivry, Liselotte, 9, **29**–34, 39
Ivry, Sidney, 34

Jerusalem, 15, 51, **52**, 59, 60
Jewish day school, 40, 45–47, 48–49, 52, 61

Jewish dietary laws, 43. *See also* kosher
Jewish Fighting Organization, 36–37
Jewish holidays, 7, 9, 10, 32: celebrating, 9, 10, 13, 20, 22, 26, 29, 31, 33, 48, 64; Purim, 32; "festival of freedom," 29, 34; Hanukkah, 48; Noce de Mimouna, 60–62; Passover, 10, 13, 15, 22, 33, 34; pilgrimage, 51; Rosh Hashanah, 42
Jewish National Fund, 40
Jewish People's and Peretz Schools, 52
Jewish traditions, **15**, 23, 39, 40, 42, 43, 45, 50, 55, 62, 64
Jonas, Rabbi Regina, 54
Joseph, Rabbi Morris, 11
Judaism, 57, 60: ultra-Orthodox, **8**, **13**, 14

Kathmandu, Nepal, 54
Kehila Jewish Community Day School, 46–**47**
karpas, green vegetable, 15, 16
kashrut, Jewish dietary laws, 43. *See also* kosher
Kaufering work camp, 26
kebabs, 60
kibbutz, 41, 52, **53**
kibbutzniks, 53
Kiddush, prayer, 15, **16**
King David High School, 48–49
kippah, skullcap, **5**, **6**, 19, **28**, 33, **52**, 55, **57**
kitl, white garment, 33
kosher, 7–8, 20, 29, 43, 46, **56**: for Passover, 20, 43, **47**, 56
kotel, wall, **51**–**52**
Kunista, Melanie, **48**

lamb: blood, 12; shank, 12, **15**, 18, 49, **56**
Lamezia Terme Jewish quarter, 56
lemon juice, 60
Leo Baeck College, 58
Lerman, Michael and Sean, **41**, 42, 43–44
Lerman, Sylvia, 40–42
liberty. *See* freedom
Lighter, Claudia, **9**, **18**, 52
Listany, Czech Republic, **29**, 30, 31

Mah Nishtanah, four questions, 16, 17, 28, **38**, 60
Maimon, Rabbi Yosef, 61
Maimonides, 61
manna, bread, 13, 18
March of the Living, The, 34, **35**
marginalization in Jewish community, 60
maror, 15, 19. *See also* bitter herbs
mass graves, 26
matzo: afikoman, **16**, 20, 38, 47, **48**; balls, **7**, 55, 60; bricks, 45–46; brittle, recipe, 37; for Passover, **22**, 26, 30, **31**, 43, 54, 55, 56; Falasha-style, 59; loksh, 30; memories of, 22, 24, 26, 30, 54, 57; origin of, 12; pancakes, 54, **61**, **62**; preparation of, **10**, **14**, 26, **37**, 49, 53; symbolism of, 15, 17, 18, 19
Mengele, Josef, Nazi doctor, 33
Merneptah, pharoah, 11
miracles, 12, 18
monotheism, 8
Montreal, 29, 34, 40–44, 50, 52, 57. Côte Saint-Luc, 7, 28, 29; Dollard-des-Ormeaux, 22, 24, 40
Montreal Food Baskets, 40–44
Morocco, 60–**63**
Moses, 11, 12, 17, 23
mufleta, pancakes, **61**

National Council of Jewish Women of Canada, 45
National Museum of American Jewish History, 40
Nazi doctor, Josef Mengele, 33
Nazi occupation, 8, 25, 26, 29, 30, 32, 33, 36–37, 39. *See also* Holocaust
Nepal, 54–55
Netherlands, 8, 53–**54**
Night, memoir, 32
Nile River, 12
Noce de Mimouna, 60–62

obligation to do good. *See also* tzedakah; volunteering
Ogus, Bram, **47**
Old Cairo, Egypt, 57
Old Testament, 43
oppression, 37, 38, 57, 64
oranges, 59–60, **61**
Orthodox Judaism, **8**, **13**

Palestine, 33, 40
Passover (Paschal): celebrating, 10, 13, 20, 22, 26, 31, 33, 48, 64; children participating in, **16**, 19; history of, 10–13; in China, 54; in Ethiopia, **58**–59; in Iraq, 59–60; in Israel, **51**–**53**; in Italy, 55–**57**; in Morocco, **60**–63; in Nepal, 54–55; in the Netherlands, 53–54; in Ukraine, 57–58; kosher for, 20, 43, **47**, 56; meaning of, 12; preparations for, **8**, **13**, **14**, **22**, **41**, **42**, **45**, 47, **52**, 55; rituals, 10, 12, 13–16, 17, 20, 38; retelling story of, 10, **11**, 14, 15, 16–19, 22–23, **28**, 33–34, **38**, 49, 50. *See also* seder
Paschal lamb. *See* lamb
payos, side curls, **8**, **13**, 14
Perestroika, 57
Perl, Moshe, 26
pestilence, 18
pharaohs, 11, **12**, 50
pilgrimage, 51
pillows, reclining on as symbol of freedom, 17, 23
plagues. *See* ten plagues
Polak, Celien, 8, **9**
Polak, Monique, author, 9, **64**
Poland, 26, 36
Popliger, Sheldon, volunteer, 42
Poussin, Nicolas, painter, 13
poverty, 42, 43, 44, 45
Prague, Czech Republic, 31, 33, 39, 40
prayers, **5**, 10, 15, **16**, 19, 20, 32, **51**, **52**
prisoners, 25, 26
promised land, 11, 12
Pumpernickel Bakery, Kathmandu, 54
purification, symbolic act of, 16, **19**. *See also* Urchatz

rabbis, 27, 32, 43, 53, 54, 58, 59–60: Aiello, Barbara, 45, 56–57; Berger, Stephen, 48–49; Bernstein, Phillip S., 23; Bykova, Elina, 42, 57–58; first female, 54; Jonas, Regina, 54; Joseph, Morris, 11; Maimon, Yosef, 61; Rodal, Leibele, 47, 48, **49**; Sicher, Gustav, 32, **33**
Ramat Yishai, 55
Ramat Yochanan, 52–**53**
recipes: charoset, **20**; chicken

soup, **49**; matzo brittle, **37**; matzo pancakes, **62**
reclining on pillows, symbol of freedom, 17, 23
Red Sea, 12, **13**, 18
religion, 8, 9, 11, 42, 55
resettlement of Jews, 9, 23, 34, 59, 61
resistance, 26, 36–37
respect, 19, 43
rituals, 10, 12, 13–16, 17, 20, 38
Rodal, Rabbi Leibele, 47, 48, **49**
Romania, 22, 24
Rosh Hashanah, 42

Sabbath (Shabbat), 24, 39, 40
salt water, 15, 16, 60
Sapinta, Romania, 22, 24, 27
Schneider, Michele, 46
school, 40, 45–47, 48–49, 52, 61
skullcap, **5**, **6**, 19, **28**, 33, **52**, 55, **57**
seder: food, **7**, 14–**15**, **22**, 24, **41**, 43, **44**, **45**, 47, **49**, **56**, 59, **61**; hamishi, 55, 57; hosting of, 9, 27, 28, 30, 33, 34, 40, **64**; in China, 54; in Ethiopia, 59; in Iraq, 60; in Israel, **53**; in Italy, 55–**57**; in Morocco, **60**–63; in Nepal, 54–55; in Ukraine, 57–58; meal, 15–17, **27**; meaning of, 14; plate, 14–**15**, **18**, 19, 49, **56**, 59–60, **61**; prayers, **16**; retelling of Passover story, 10, 14, 16–19, 22–23, **28**, 33–34, **38**, 49, 50; sharing of, 16, 26, **27**, 30, 39, 40, 41, 51
Seder on Top of the World, The, 54–55
seniors' facilities, 39, 40, 44, 48, 49
Sephardic Jews, 60
shank bone, lamb, 12, **15**, 18, 49, **56**
Shapira, Amit Asher, 55
sharing with less fortunate, 16, 30, 39, 40–44, 45, 46, **49**. *See also* charity; tzedakah; volunteering
Shoah, 36. *See also* Holocaust
Sicher, Rabbi Gustav, 32, **33**
slavery, 10, 11, 12, 15, 16, 17
Soviet Jews, 57–58
Spier, Jozef L., **54**
starvation, 26, 36, 49
Sudetenland, 30
suffering, 17, 18, 27
superstitions, 62
symbolism, 10, 14–15, 16, 17, 18, 20, 44, 59, 60, 62
synagogues, 7, 24, 29, 32, 37, **54**, 57, 59

Temples of Jerusalem, 15, **52**, 58
ten plagues, 11, 12, 17–**18**
Tet Ghetto, **25**
thankfulness. *See* gratitude
Theresienstadt concentration camp, 32
Tiefstack concentration camp, 33
Torah, 59
traditions, **15**, 23, 39, 40, 42, 43, 45, 50, 55, 62, 64
Treblinka death camp, 36
Tucson Jewish Food Festival, 55
tzaddikim, 39, 40
tzedakah, 39, **40**, 41, 44, **46**, **47**, 48. *See also* charity; sharing with less fortunate; volunteering
tzedakah box, **40**, **46**, **47**

Ukraine, 42, 57–58
Union of Soviet Socialist Republics (USSR), 57
Urchatz, washing of the hands, 15–16, 17, **19**

Vaihingen concentration camp, 26
volunteering, 39, 40–44, 45, **48**, **49**

Wailing Wall. *See* Western Wall
washing hands. *See* Urchatz
Warsaw Ghetto Uprising, 26, 33, 36–37
Western Wall, **5**, **51**, **52**, **58**
wine, 10, 15, 16, 18, 19, 20, 26
Wiesel, Elie, author, 32
Wirtis, John, chef, 55
World War II, 23, 26, 33, 34. *See also* Holocaust

Yachatz, 16
Yad Vashem memorial, 31
yarmulke. *See* kippah
Younger, Benzion, 9, **22**–23, **24**–28, 34

Zydowska Organizacja Bojowa (ZOB). *See* Jewish Fighting Organization

Acknowledgments

Thanks to the many people who agreed to be interviewed for this book. Special thanks to Ben Younger and Liselotte Ivry, who spoke candidly to me about their experiences during the Holocaust. Thanks also to my mom, Celien Polak, and to Deena Sacks Creatchman, Sylvia Lerman, Michael Lerman, Sean Lerman, Sheldon Popliger, David Guttman, Glenda Ephron Cooper, Michele Schneider, Bram Ogus, Rabbi Leibele Rodal, Rabbi Stephen Berger, Nira Friedman, Amit Asher Shapira, Rabbi Barbara Aiello, Rabbi Elina Bykova and Susannah Heschel for sharing your stories and teaching me so much about Passover. Thank you to Benjamin Ickovich (and his parents Avi and Nora Ickovich) for participating in a photo shoot for the cover. Thanks to Robin Stevenson, who read early drafts of this book, to Betsy Gray who checked the manuscript for errors and to my smart and sensitive editor Sarah Harvey.